History Snapshots

The Victorians

Sarah Ridley

W
FRANKLIN WATTS
LONDON • SYDNEY

This edition 2011.

First published in 2007 by
Franklin Watts
338 Euston Road
London NW1 3BH

Franklin Watts Australia
Level 17/207 Kent Street
Sydney, NSW 2000

Series editor: Sarah Peutrill
Art director: Jonathan Hair
Design: Jane Hawkins

A CIP catalogue record for this book is available from the
British Library.

Dewey number: 941.081

ISBN: 978 1 4451 0581 9

Printed in China

Picture credits:
Colchester Museum: 10b, 14, 15t, 18b, 28t
English Heritage NMR: 17t, 19.
Mary Evans Picture Library: 3, 6.
Henry Guttmann/Hulton Archive/Getty Images: 25t.
Hulton Archive/Getty Images: 22, 27t.
Oliver Green/TfL: 21b.
Lancashire County Library & Information Service: 12t.
Leeds Library & Information Service: 10t, 16t.
Museum of English Rural Life, Reading: 8b, 9, 17b, 18t.
NMPFT/Science & Society Picture Library: 20, 24, 26b
Kodak Collection.
Oldham Local Studies & Archives: 12b, 13, 16b.
Science Museum/Science & Society Picture Library: 23.
Ann Ronan Picture Library / HIP / TopFoto : 26t.

Thanks to the following for kind permission to use their
photographs in this publication: Lionel Baker 8t, 21t; the
Lee family 11; the Ridley family 15b, 25b, 28b

Every attempt has been made to clear copyright. Should
there be any inadvertent omission please apply to the
publisher for rectification.

Franklin Watts is a division of Hachette Children's Books,
an Hachette UK company.
www.hachette.co.uk

Daisy Daisy,
Give me your answer do!
I'm half crazy,
All for the love of you!
It won't be a stylish marriage,
I can't afford a carriage,
But you'll look sweet on the seat
Of a bicycle built for two!
    Victorian music hall song by Harry Dacre, 1892

Contents

Who were the Victorians?

The people who lived in Britain during the reign of Queen Victoria are called the Victorians. Queen Victoria reigned from 1837 to 1901, longer than any other British king or queen.

Date: c. 1860

In the centre stand Queen Victoria and her husband, Prince Albert. They are surrounded by their nine children. Many Victorians had large families of eight or nine children.

Victorian timeline

1837 Victoria becomes queen at the age of 18.

1840 Queen Victoria marries Albert.

1844 By law, the Factory Act reduces the number of hours that children between the ages of 8 and 13 can work. Various Factory Acts slowly improve working conditions.

1854–56 The Crimean War.

1861 Prince Albert dies.

1863 The first underground train is built in London.

1870 The government builds many schools.

1887 Britain celebrates Queen Victoria's Golden Jubilee (50 years as queen).

1891 Primary education becomes free for all children under the age of 12.

1897 Britain celebrates Queen Victoria's Diamond Jubilee (60 years as queen).

1901 Queen Victoria dies at the age of 81.

Life in the countryside

When Victoria became queen, most people lived in the countryside and worked on farms. Their wages were low, so many farm workers moved to towns to find higher-paid jobs.

Date: 1895

Mr Baker, a farmer and mill owner, and his sister, lived in this house. Miss Baker had servants to clean and cook for her.

Date: c. 1864

Mrs Wickham and her children gather outside their cottage. She worked all day – cleaning, washing clothes, growing vegetables and cooking for the family.

Date: 1901

Farm workers load carts with hay. Men, women and children worked in the fields during the harvest.

Be a history detective

- Why did so many people work in the fields compared with today?
- How do the carts move?
- The windmill is grinding corn to make flour. What makes it work?

Town and city life

Towns and cities grew during Victorian times as people came to find work in factories, shops and offices. Many places struggled to cope. The streets were dirty and diseases spread easily. From the 1860s, town and city councils made improvements.

Date: 1890

These homes in Leeds were damp, cramped and badly built. Many had more than one family to each house.

A well-off family sits on the steps of their home. Some families could afford to move to new homes on the edge of towns and cities.

Date: c. 1870s

Date: c. 1900

An ironmonger stands outside his shop. Many Victorians became shopkeepers, selling goods and food to people living in towns and cities.

Be a history detective

- Look for the building at the end of the street in the 1890 photo. It is the shared toilet (privy) for the whole street.

- Find the following in the window display of the ironmonger's shop: a bicycle, tools, watering cans and bird cages.

Victorian factories

Victorian factories produced all sorts of goods, from cloth, to engine parts, to brooms. While factory owners grew rich, their workers earned little money and worked long hours using dangerous machinery.

Date: 1890s

Factory workers stop for a moment in a cotton-weaving factory. Many factories and mills in the north of England made cloth.

A boy cleans a cotton-spinning machine. Factory owners liked to employ child workers because they paid them less than adult workers. Also, their small hands could reach into the machines.

Date: c. 1880s

Men and boys gather outside the factory where they make gas meters. Slowly the law changed to stop young children from working in factories and to make machinery safer for all factory workers.

Date: c. 1870s

Be a history detective

- Look at how closely packed the machinery is in the weaving factory. Imagine how noisy it must have been when all the machines were working.
- How old do you think the boys are in the gas meter factory?
- Find out what other jobs Victorian children did.

Family life

Wherever Victorians lived, the family and the home were very important. While poorer families spent most of their days working, wealthier families had more time to relax.

Date: c. 1880s

Many families made their own fun by playing music together, reading, sewing and playing games.

A family gathering. The father was the head of the family and his wife looked after the home and the children.

Date: c. 1895

A lady takes tea in her garden. Well-off Victorians loved to visit each other for cups of tea and a chat.

Date: c. 1890s

Be a history detective

- Look at what people are wearing in these photos and compare them to the clothes people wear today.

- Visit a local museum to find out more about Victorian life in your area.

In and out of school

When Victoria became queen, few children went to school. Slowly this changed as the government built new schools. When children were not at school or work, they played with whatever toys they had.

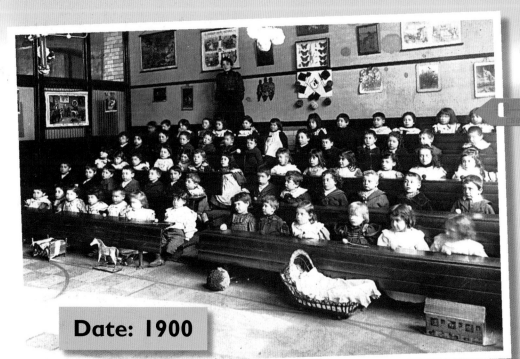

Pupils sit in rows at their desks. Victorian children learnt by repeating and remembering facts.

Date: 1900

Children play in the school yard. Children wrote on slates, like the one on the boy's back (far right).

Date: 1880s

Children show off their homemade carts. Poorer children played with skipping ropes, spinning tops and homemade toys.

Date: 1901

Date: 1897

Wealthy children had plenty to play with. Parents bought them puzzles, books, games, dolls and trains for inside and bicycles and tennis rackets for outside.

Be a history detective

- How many children can you count in the infant classroom?
- What toys can you see in the classroom?
- What are the children doing in their playtime?

Time off

The Victorians began to have more free time. Some people joined sports clubs, while others visited new parks, museums or theatres. Those who could afford it, visited the seaside.

Seaside holidays became very popular during Victorian times.

Date: 1898

Families visit the park. Many towns and cities created new parks, with boating lakes, gardens and big spaces to play in.

Date: 1890s

Everyone is watching the girls dance around the Maypole. People enjoyed fairs, walks and special events at Christmas, Easter and other religious holidays.

Date: 1897

Be a history detective

- How did the Victorians dress for the beach? Find out more about Victorian seaside holidays.
- Find the building on the hill in the park. It is a bandstand, where musicians performed concerts.

Getting about

The Victorians used the first bicycles, trams and cars. Railway engineers built railway tracks so that people and goods could travel on trains between towns and cities.

Date: c. 1880

Steam trains pass at a tiny Welsh railway station. Many Victorian railway bridges, tunnels and stations are still in use today.

Be a history detective

- Look for steam coming out of the train funnel. These trains burnt coal to make them move.
- Can you find the tram lines (rails) on the city streets (right)?

People travelled by pony and trap, especially in the countryside.

Date: 1895

Date: 1895

In towns and cities, people paid to ride on horse-drawn trams, buses and in cabs (another name for taxis).

Victorian inventions

There were many new inventions in Britain during Victorian times. They included the postage stamp, invented by Rowland Hill, modern photography, invented by William Fox Talbot, and one of the first ever light bulbs, invented by Joseph Swan.

The son of John Dunlop, who invented the air-filled (pneumatic) bicycle tyre, shows off his father's invention.

Date: 1888

Guglielmo Marconi, an Italian who moved to London, discovered how to send messages through the air along invisible radio waves.

Date: 1900

Be a history detective

- Compare the 1888 bicycle with the penny farthing on page 28. Which bicycle would you like to ride?
- Use the Internet to find out more about the inventors mentioned on these pages.

The British Empire

Queen Victoria ruled over a huge empire stretching around the world. It included Australia, India, Canada and countries in Africa (see page 29 for details). Many Victorians left Britain to work in these countries, or to settle there for life.

A wealthy family relax in their garden in Canada. While some settlers grew rich, others found life very hard.

Date: 1860

British settlers in Australia, surrounded by their Aborigine workers. In many cases, people already lived in the lands that British people took over.

Date: 1855

Date: 1890s

British and Indian army soldiers pose for the camera. Some Victorians went to India to be in the army, or to work for the government.

Be a history detective

- Find out whether any of your family worked in the British Empire, or settled abroad during Victorian times.
- What game have the family in Canada been playing?

Life improves

By the time Queen Victoria died in 1901, working conditions had improved for many. Towns and cities were healthier, hospitals were cleaner and some of the worst housing had been replaced.

Sir Joseph Bazalgette designed and organised the building of proper sewers under the streets of London. The sewers improved the health of Londoners by taking away dirty water that often caused illnesses.

Date: 1877

Lord Ashley, also known as the Earl of Shaftesbury or Lord Shaftesbury. Alongside other politicians, Lord Ashley helped to make the laws that improved the lives of working people.

Date: 1876

Florence Nightingale sits in the centre, surrounded by nurses. She worked all her life to improve hospitals and nursing.

Date: 1886

Date: 1880s

Children relax outside one of the homes built by the owners of the Cadbury chocolate factory. The homes were better than most workers' homes at the time.

Be a history detective

- Find a picture of a nurse in uniform today. How has the uniform changed since the 1886 picture?
- What is the young girl on the left playing with in the 1880s picture?

The new photography

Photography was invented in the 1830s. The Victorians loved this new way of recording their lives. Many people visited photographers' studios to have their picture taken. Look at …

William Brown

the owner of a penny farthing bicycle …

Amy St Leger

the lady in her best clothes …

Lily, Berty and Ada Ridley

and the boy with his sisters.

Glossary

Aborigine People living in Australia when Europeans arrived.

Act A rule made by the government. The Factory Acts are rules relating to the running of factories in Britain.

British Empire The countries ruled by Britain. During Queen Victoria's reign, the British Empire included countries stretching from New Zealand and Australia, through India and Sri Lanka to South Africa, Kenya and Nigeria, to Canada and islands in the Caribbean.

Council The people who organise street lighting, rubbish collection, housing, drainage etc for a town, city or district.

Factory A building where goods are made.

Gas meter A machine that keeps track of the amount of gas used by a household or business.

Ironmonger A skilled worker who makes all sorts of objects out of iron.

Law The rules that govern a country.

Maypole A pole painted with flowers and ribbons, for dancing around on May Day (1st May).

Penny farthing A type of bicycle with a very large front wheel and a small back one, named after coins of the day.

Settler A person who goes to live in a new country or place.

Sewers A network of underground pipes which carry dirty water away to rivers or treatment works.

Slate A school slate in Victorian times was a piece of slate stone in a wood frame which children used to write on with a sharp piece of slate.

Studio (photographer's) The room at a photographer's workplace where he takes photos of people.

Tram A vehicle, like a bus, that runs on tracks called tram lines.

Trap A two-wheeled carriage.

Index

Further information

Books
Starting History: The Victorians by Sally Hewitt (Franklin Watts)

A Victorian Childhood series by Ruth Thomson (Franklin Watts)

Websites
www.bbc.co.uk/schools/victorians/
On this interactive website you can learn about Victorian children's lives at work, at school and at play.

www.bbc.co.uk/schools/famouspeople/
Choose from Brunel, Fry, Nightingale or Seacole to find out about the lives of some famous Victorians.

www.victorians.org.uk/
An excellent website about Victorians created by Tiverton Museum.

Note to parents and teachers: Every effort has been made by the Publishers to ensure that these websites are suitable for children, that they are of the highest educational value, and that they contain no inappropriate or offensive material. However, because of the nature of the Internet, it is impossible to guarantee that the contents of these sites will not be altered. We strongly advise that Internet access is supervised by a responsible adult.